ESSENTIAL ELEMENTS®

Audio Access Included

GUITAR SONGS

MID BEGINNER

POWER CHORD ROCK

T0081843

PLAYBACK+
Speed • Pitch • Balance • Loop

To access audio visit:
www.halleonard.com/mylibrary

Enter Code
8491-1513-3744-2138

ISBN: 978-1-4234-3343-9

HAL•LEONARD®

Visit Hal Leonard Online at
www.halleonard.com

Contact Us:
Hal Leonard
7777 West Bluemound Road
Milwaukee, WI 53213
Email: info@halleonard.com

In Europe contact:
Hal Leonard Europe Limited
Distribution Centre, Newmarket Road
Bury St Edmunds, Suffolk, IP33 3YB
Email: info@halleonardeurope.com

In Australia contact:
Hal Leonard Australia Pty. Ltd.
4 Lentara Court
Cheltenham, Victoria, 3192 Australia
Email: info@halleonard.com.au

CONTENTS

ALL THE SMALL THINGS

Words and Music by Tom De Longe and Mark Hoppus

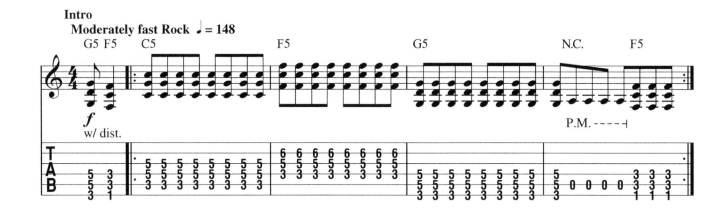

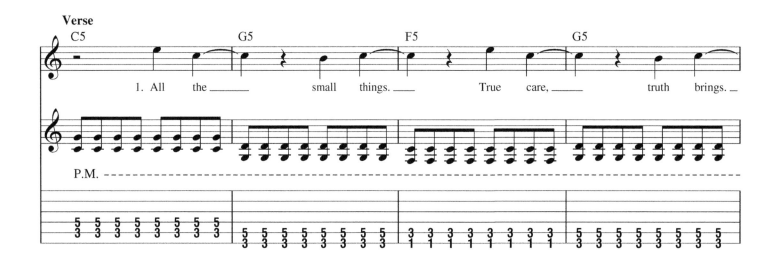

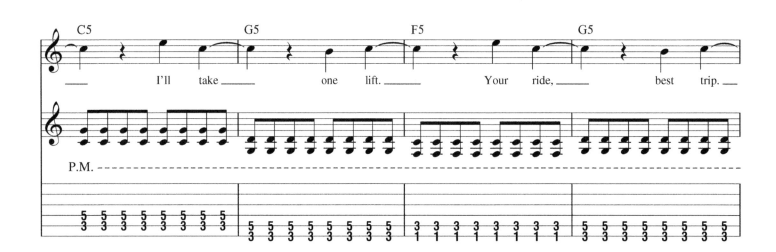

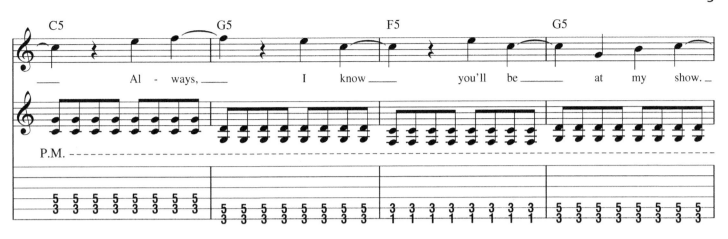

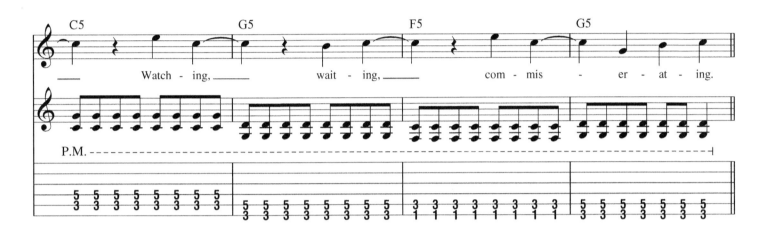

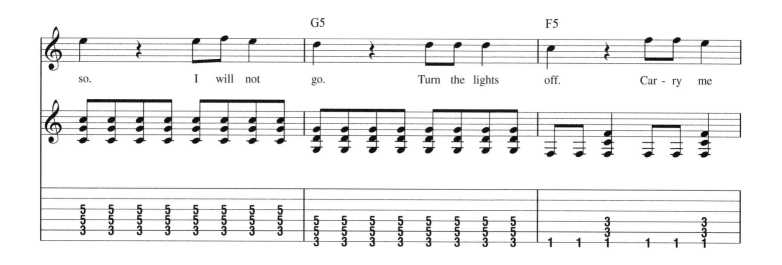

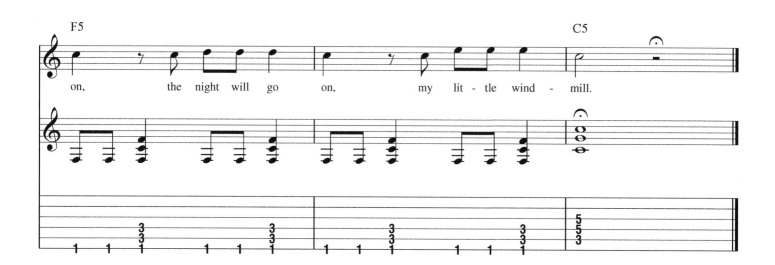

I LOVE ROCK 'N ROLL

Words and Music by Alan Merrill and Jake Hooker

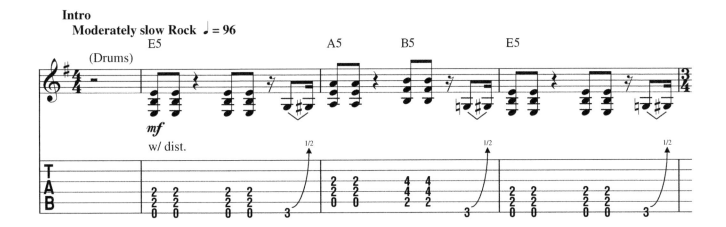

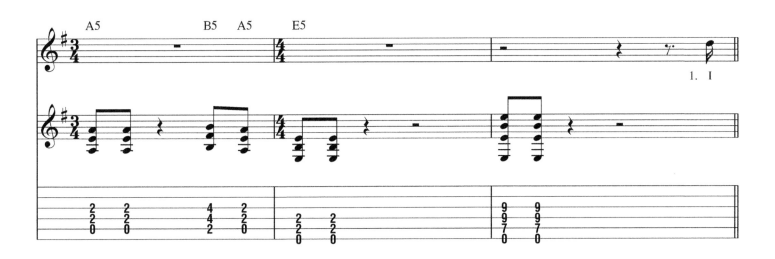

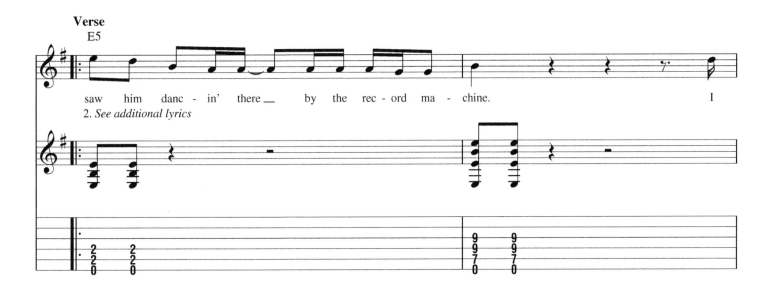

Chorus

Pre-Chorus

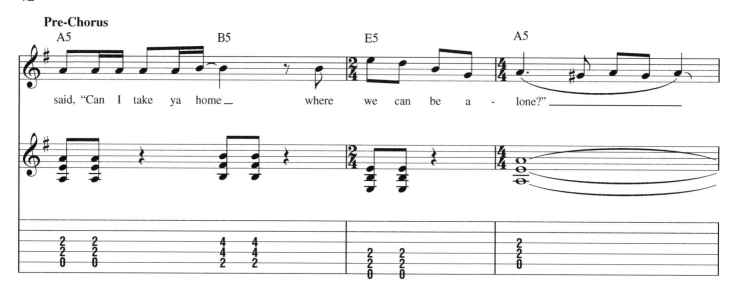

said, "Can I take ya home ___ where we can be a - lone?" _____

Next, we were mov - in' on, ___ he was with me, yeah, me! And we'll be

mov - in' on, ___ and sing - in' that same old song, yeah, with me. ___ Sing - in',

Breakdown-Chorus

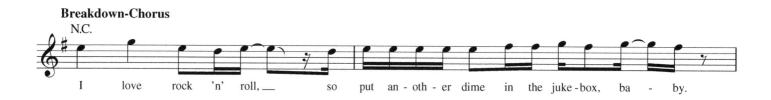

I love rock 'n' roll, ___ so put an - oth - er dime in the juke - box, ba - by.

I love rock 'n' roll, ___ so come and take your time and dance with me.

Outro-Chorus

I love rock 'n' roll, __ so put an-oth-er dime in the juke-box, ba - by.

1., 2., 3.

I love rock and roll, __ so come and take your time and dance with...

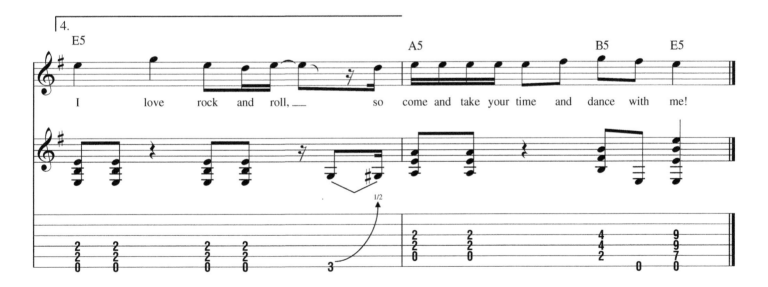

4.

I love rock and roll, __ so come and take your time and dance with me!

Additional Lyrics

2. He smiled, so I got up and asked for his name.
   "That don't matter," he said, "'cause it's all the same."
   I said, "Can I take ya home where we can be alone?"
   And next, we were movin' on, he was with me, yeah, me!
   Next, we were movin' on, he was with me, yeah, me, singin'...

I WON'T BACK DOWN

Words and Music by Tom Petty and Jeff Lynne

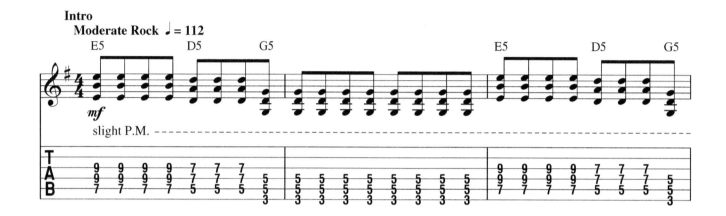

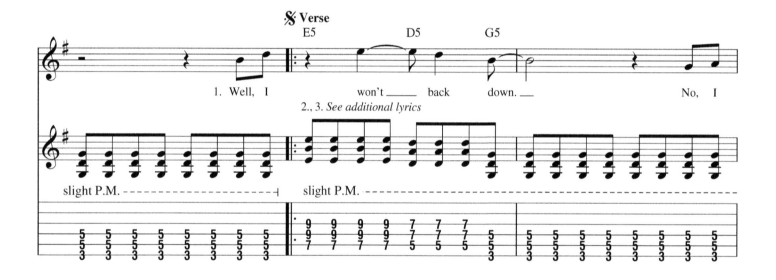

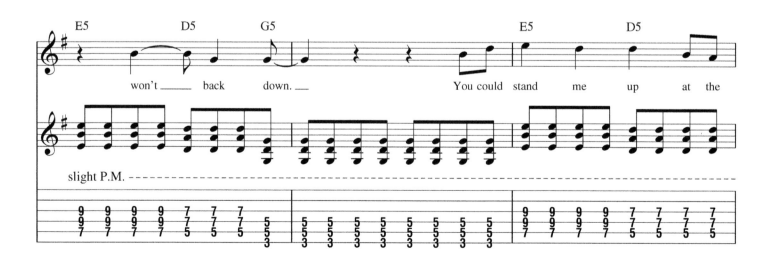

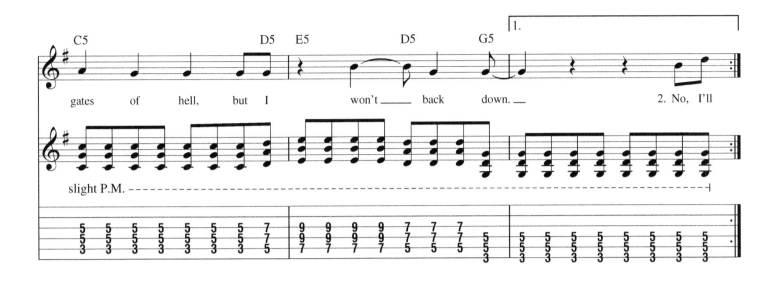

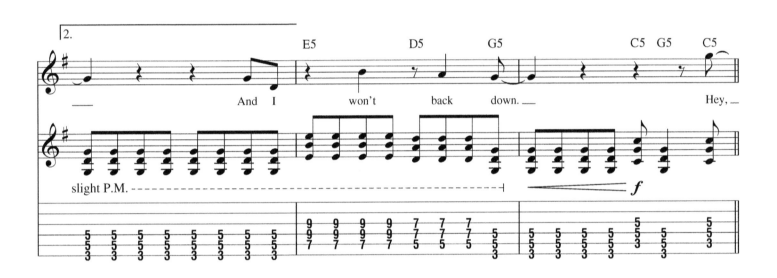

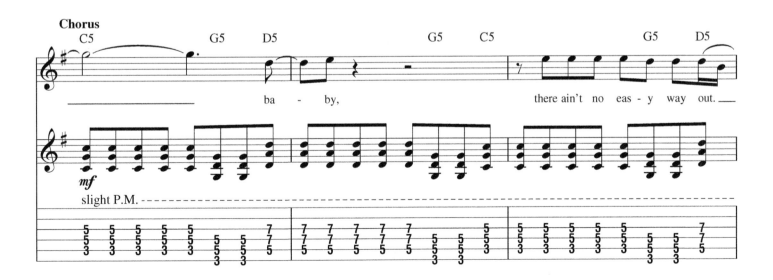

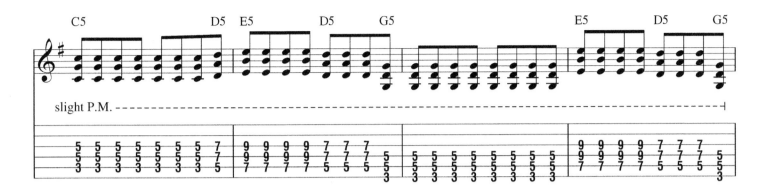

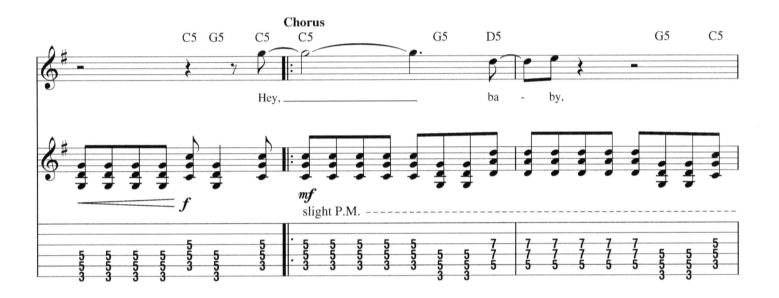

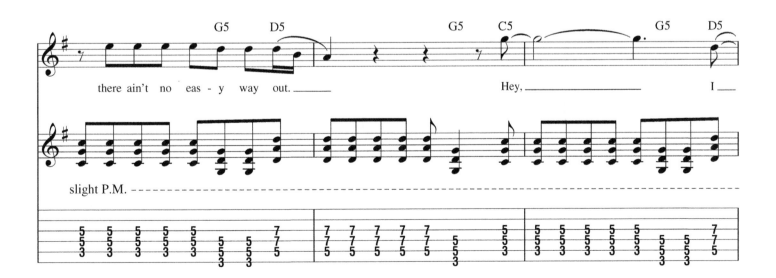

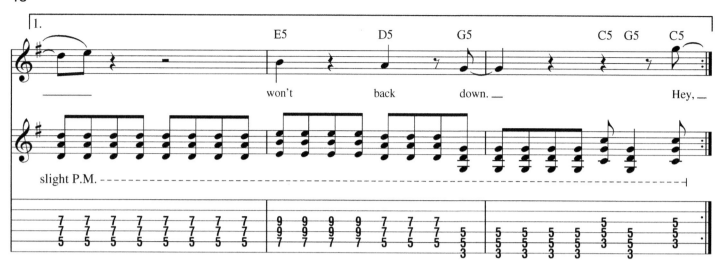

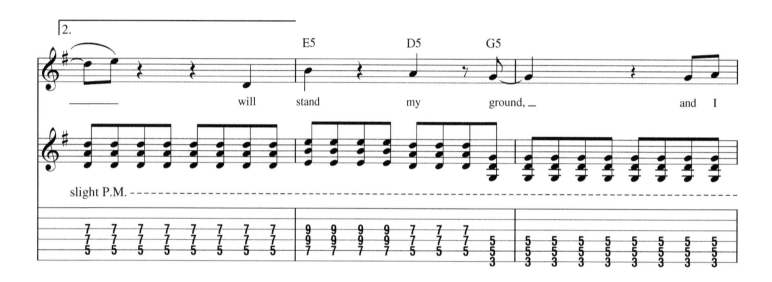

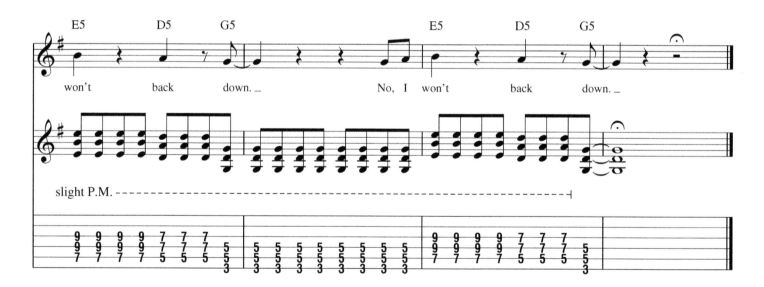

Additional Lyrics

2. No, I'll stand my ground.
   Won't be turned around.
   And I'll keep this world from draggin' me down,
   Gonna stand my ground.
   And I won't back down.

3. Well, I know what's right.
   I got just one life
   In a world that keeps on pushin' me around.
   But I'll stand my ground,
   And I won't back down.

MONY, MONY

Words and Music by Bobby Bloom, Tommy James, Ritchie Cordell and Bo Gentry

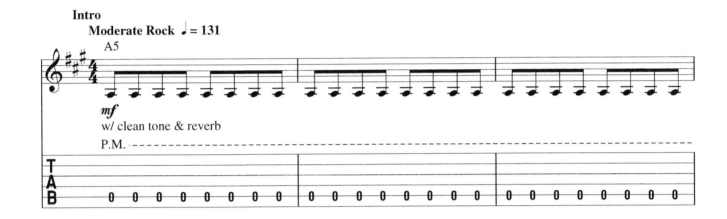

1. Here ___ she come now, say - in', "Mo - ny, Mo - ny." ___
2. *See additional lyrics*

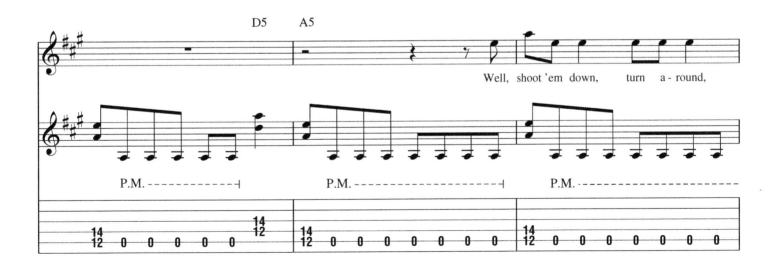

Well, shoot 'em down, turn a - round,

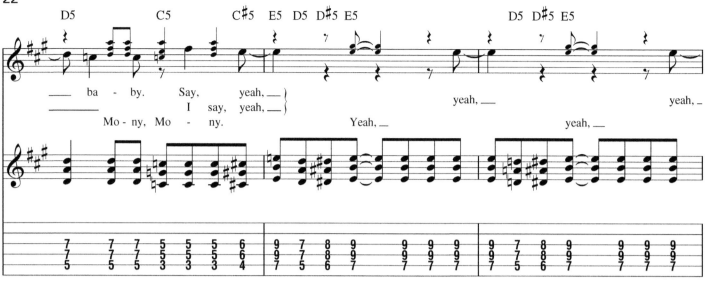

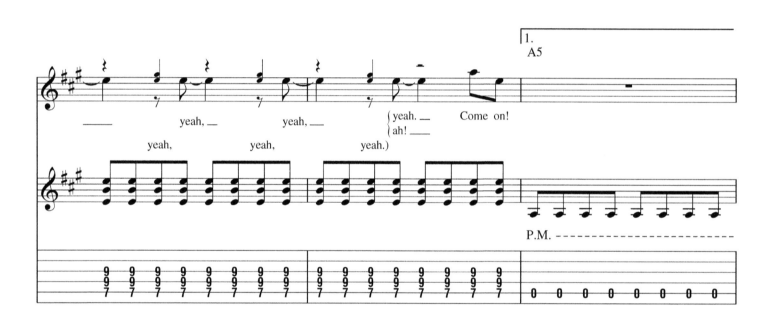

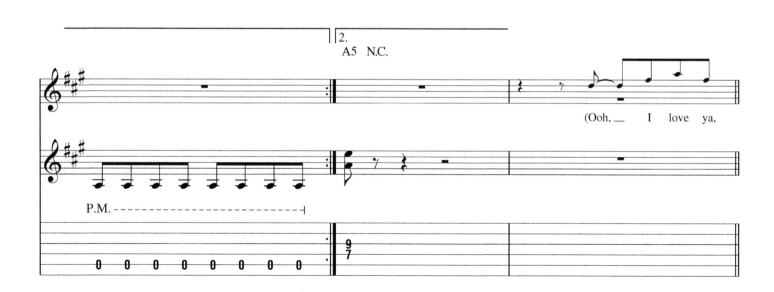

Breakdown

So good. __

Mo - ny, Mo - Mo - Mo - ny.   Ooh, __ I love ya, Mo - ny, Mo - Mo - Mo -

So   fine. __   Al - right. ____

- ny.   Ooh, __ I love ya, Mo - ny, Mo - Mo - Mo - ny.   Ooh, ____ I love ya,

E5 D5   D#5 E5

Say, Mo - ny, Mo - ny.   Yeah, __   ev - 'ry - bod -

Mo - ny, Mo - ny.   Yeah, __

D5   D#5 E5

y,   y - yeah, __   yeah, __   yeah, __   yeah. __

yeah, __   yeah,   yeah,   wah!)

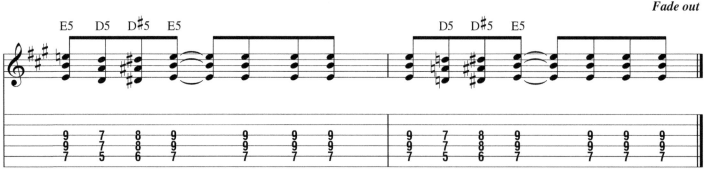

Additional Lyrics

2. Wake me, shake me, Mony, Mony.
   Shotgun, get it done. Come on, Mony.
   Don't 'cha stop cookin', it feels so good, yeah.
   Hey! Well, but don't stop now, hey,
   Come on, Mony. Well, come on, Mony.

ROCK YOU LIKE A HURRICANE

Words and Music by Herman Rarebell, Klaus Meine and Rudolf Schenker

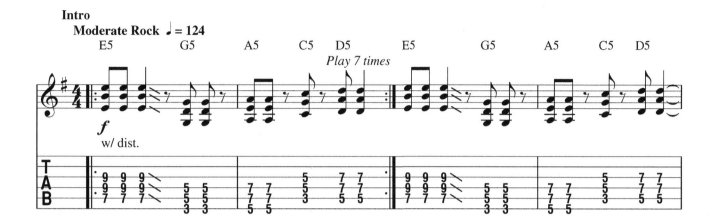

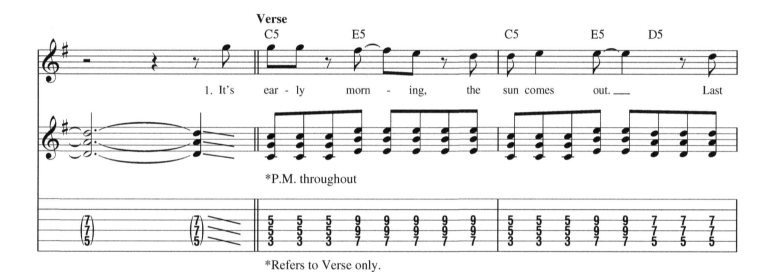

*Refers to Verse only.

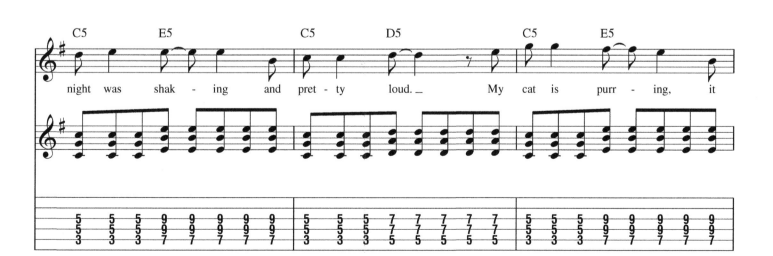

*Rub the edge of the pick down the strings, producing a scratchy sound.

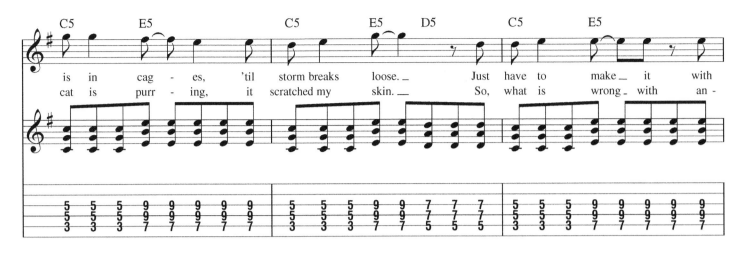

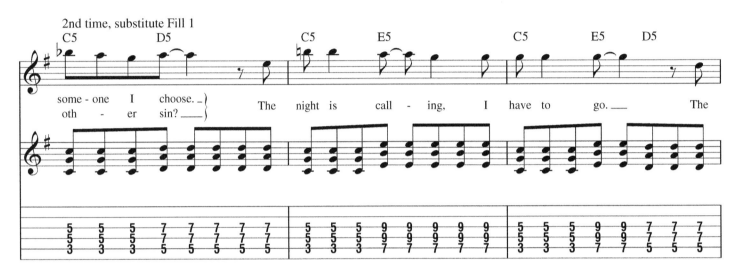

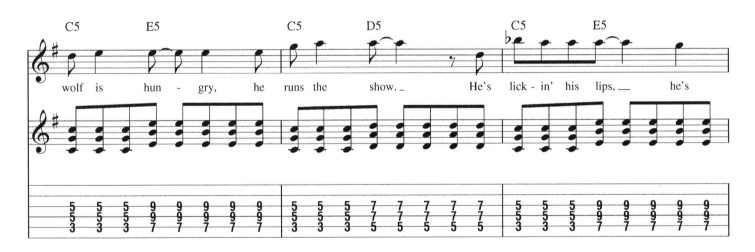

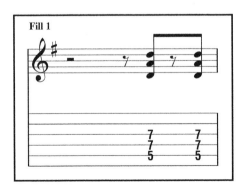

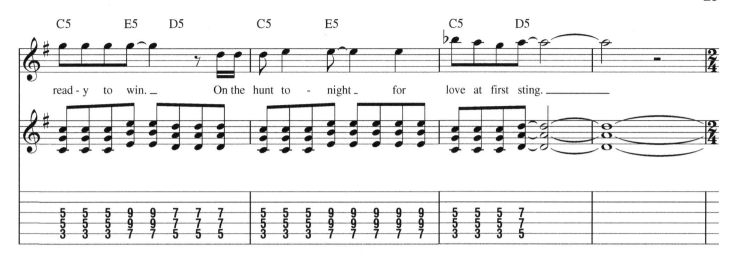

ready to win. _ On the hunt to - night _ for love at first sting. _____

Chorus

Here I am, rock _ you like a hur - ri - cane.

To Coda ⊕

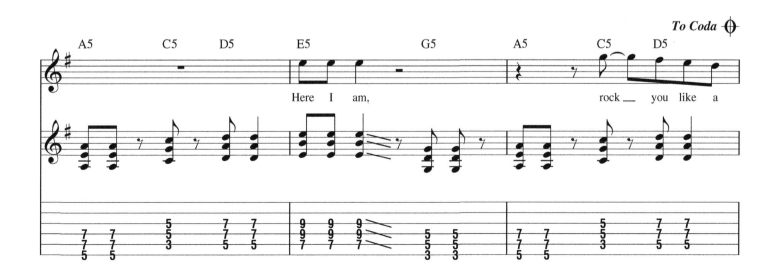

Here I am, rock _ you like a

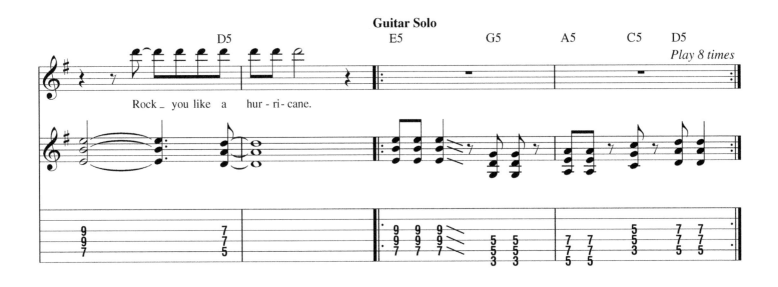

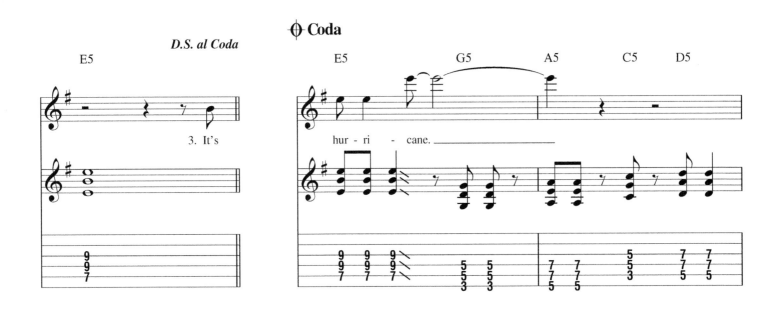

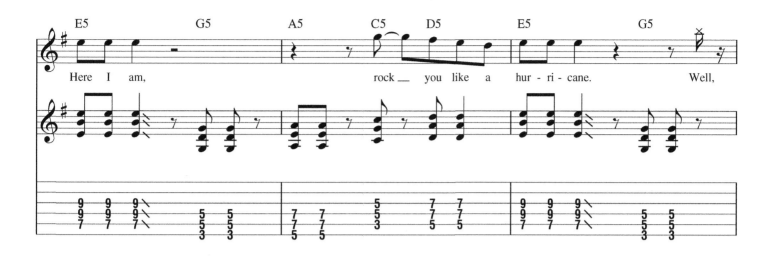

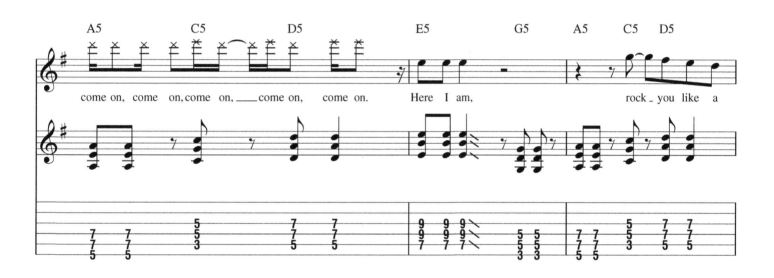

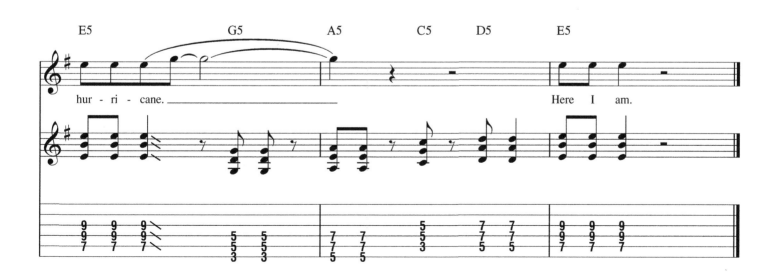

SELF ESTEEM

Words and Music by Dexter Holland

Verse

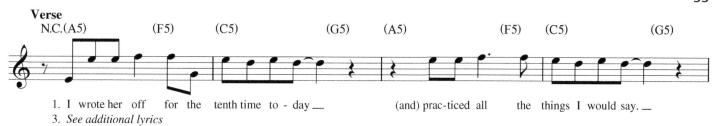

1. I wrote her off for the tenth time to-day __ (and) prac-ticed all the things I would say. __
3. *See additional lyrics*

But she came o-ver, I lost my nerve. __ I took her back and made her des-sert. __

Pre-Chorus

(Now) I __ know __ I'm be-in' used. __ That's o-kay, man,'cause I
See additional lyrics

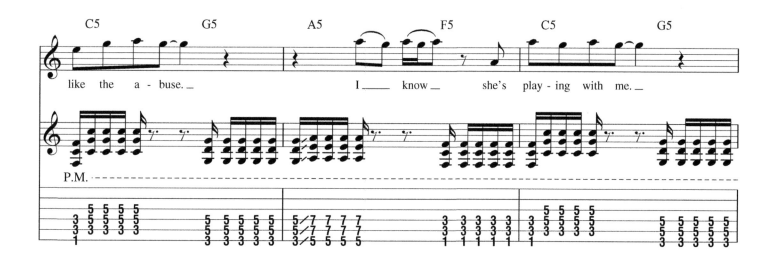

like the a-buse. __ I __ know __ she's play-ing with me. __

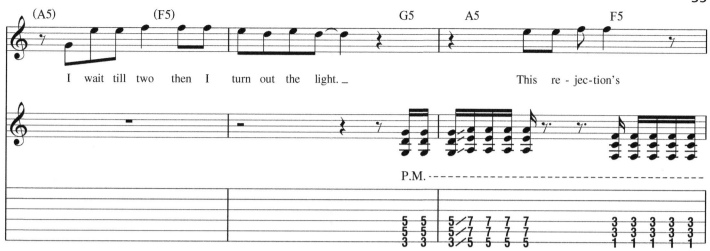

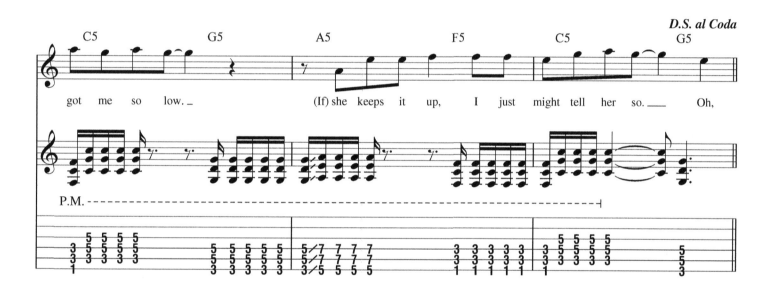

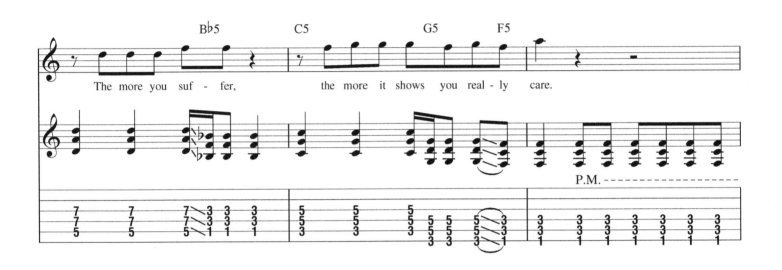

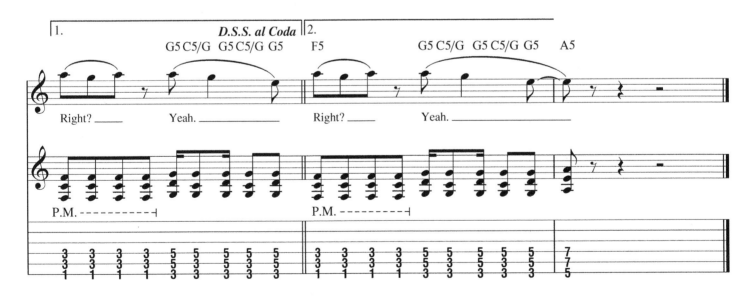

Additional Lyrics

3. Now I'll relate this little bit
That happens more than I'd like to admit.
Late at night she knocks on my door.
She's drunk again and looking to score.

Pre-Chorus (Now) I know I should say no,
But that's kind of hard when she's ready to go.
I may be dumb but I'm not a dweeb.
I'm just a sucker with no self-esteem.

SMELLS LIKE TEEN SPIRIT

Words and Music by Kurt Cobain, Krist Novoselic and Dave Grohl

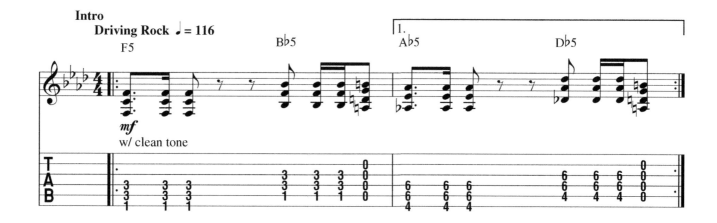

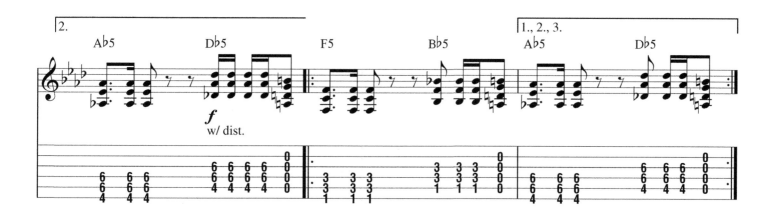

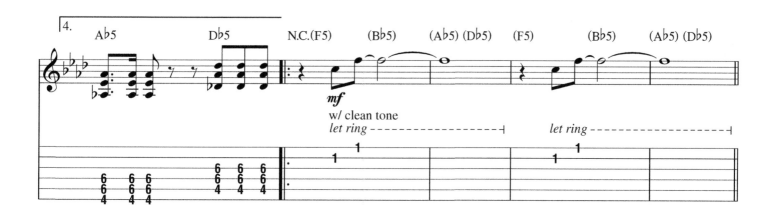

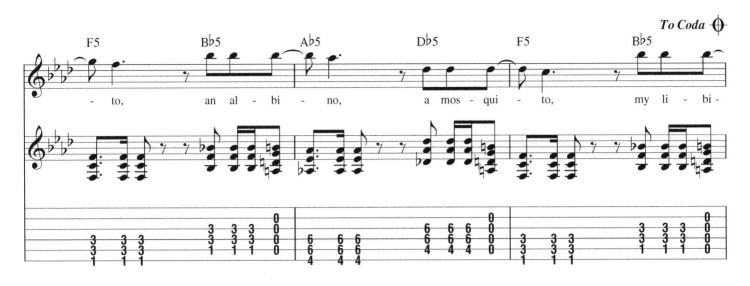

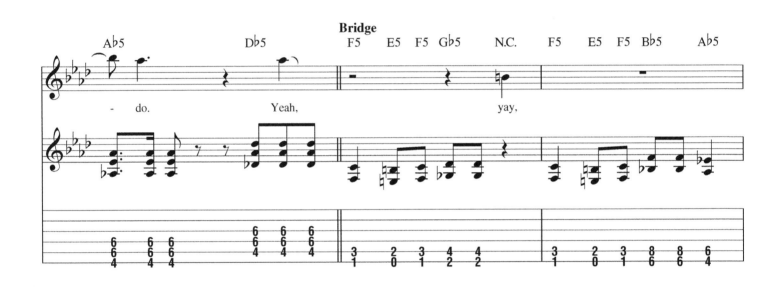

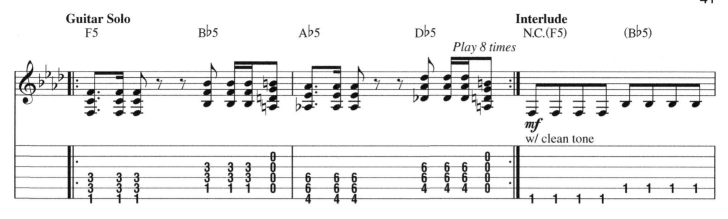

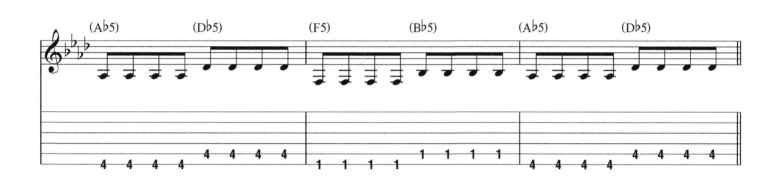

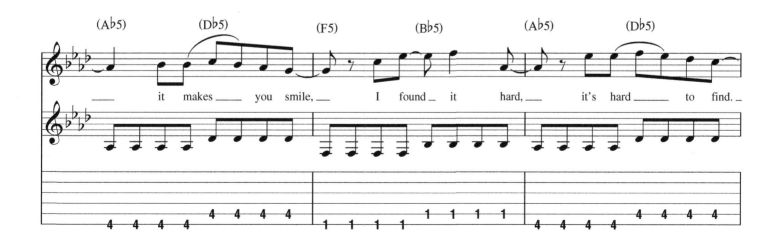

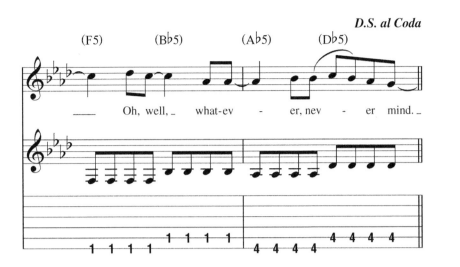

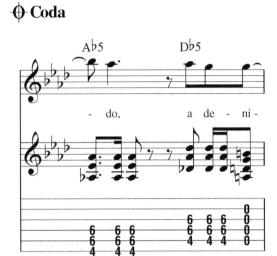

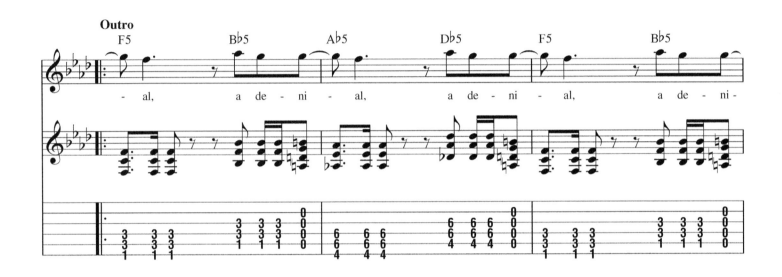

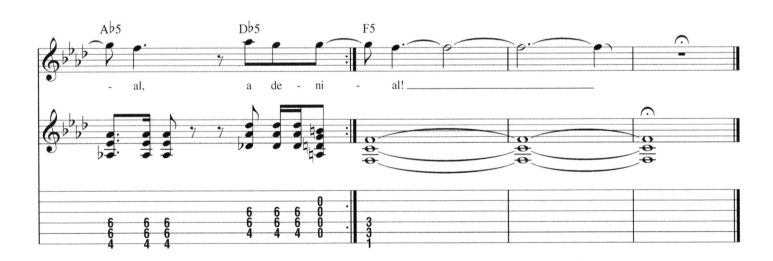

Additional Lyrics

2. I'm worse at what I do best,
   And for this gift I feel blessed.
   Our little group has always been
   And always will until the end.

YOU REALLY GOT ME

Words and Music by Ray Davies

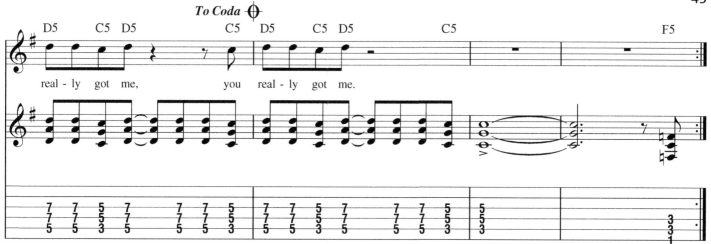

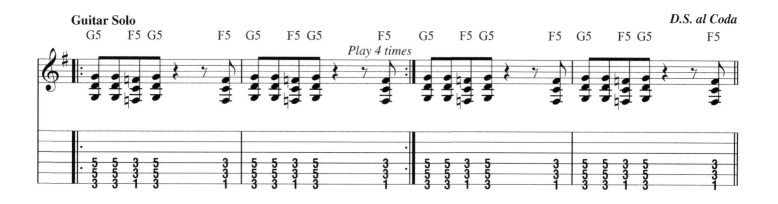

Additional Lyrics

2., 3. See, don't ever set me free,
I always wanna be by your side.
Girl, you really got me now,
You got me so I can't sleep at night.

Guitar Notation Legend

Guitar music can be notated two different ways: on a *musical staff*, and in *tablature*.

THE MUSICAL STAFF shows pitches and rhythms and is divided by bar lines into measures. Pitches are named after the first seven letters of the alphabet.

TABLATURE graphically represents the guitar fingerboard. Each horizontal line represents a string, and each number represents a fret.

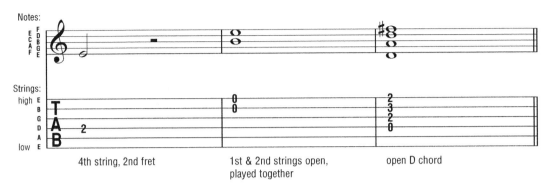

4th string, 2nd fret | 1st & 2nd strings open, played together | open D chord

CHORD DIAGRAMS graphically represent the guitar fretboard to show correct chord fingerings.

- The letter above the diagram tells the name of the chord.
- The top, bold horizontal line represents the nut of the guitar. Each thin horizontal line represents a fret. Each vertical line represents a string; the low E string is on the far left and the high E string is on the far right.
- A dot shows where to put your fret-hand finger and the number at the bottom of the diagram tells which finger to use.
- The "O" above the string means play it open, while an "✕" means don't play the string.

Definitions for Special Guitar Notation

HALF-STEP BEND: Strike the note and bend up 1/2 step.

WHOLE-STEP BEND: Strike the note and bend up one step.

MUFFLED STRINGS: A percussive sound is produced by laying the fret hand across the string(s) without depressing, and striking them with the pick hand.

PALM MUTING: The note is partially muted by the pick hand lightly touching the string(s) just before the bridge.

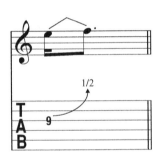

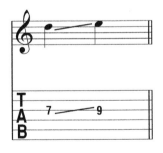

HAMMER-ON: Strike the first (lower) note with one finger, then sound the higher note (on the same string) with another finger by fretting it without picking.

PULL-OFF: Place both fingers on the notes to be sounded. Strike the first note and without picking, pull the finger off to sound the second (lower) note.

LEGATO SLIDE: Strike the first note and then slide the same fret-hand finger up or down to the second note. The second note is not struck.

SHIFT SLIDE: Same as legato slide, except the second note is struck.

Additional Musical Definitions

Fill
- Label used to identify a brief melodic figure which is to be inserted into the arrangement.

D.S. al Coda
- Go back to the sign (𝄋), then play until the measure marked "*To Coda*," then skip to the section labelled "**Coda.**"

D.C. al Fine
- Go back to the beginning of the song and play until the measure marked "*Fine*" (end).

N.C.
- No chord. Instrument is silent.

- Repeat measures between signs.

- When a repeated section has different endings, play the first ending only the first time and the second ending only the second time.

HAL•LEONARD GUITAR PLAY-ALONG

This series will help you play your favorite songs quickly and easily. Just follow the tab and listen to the audio to the hear how the guitar should sound, and then play along using the separate backing tracks. Audio files also include software to slow down the tempo without changing pitch. The melody and lyrics are included in the book so that you can sing or simply follow along.

INCLUDES TAB

Complete song lists available online.

VOL. 1 – ROCK	00699570 / $17.99	
VOL. 2 – ACOUSTIC	00699569 / $16.99	
VOL. 3 – HARD ROCK	00699573 / $17.99	
VOL. 4 – POP/ROCK	00699571 / $16.99	
VOL. 5 – THREE CHORD SONGS	00300985 / $16.99	
VOL. 6 – '90S ROCK	00298615 / $16.99	
VOL. 7 – BLUES	00699575 / $19.99	
VOL. 8 – ROCK	00699585 / $16.99	
VOL. 9 – EASY ACOUSTIC SONGS	00151708 / $16.99	
VOL. 10 – ACOUSTIC	00699586 / $16.95	
VOL. 11 – EARLY ROCK	00699579 / $15.99	
VOL. 12 – ROCK POP	00291724 / $17.99	
VOL. 14 – BLUES ROCK	00699582 / $16.99	
VOL. 15 – R&B	00699583 / $17.99	
VOL. 16 – JAZZ	00699584 / $16.99	
VOL. 17 – COUNTRY	00699588 / $17.99	
VOL. 18 – ACOUSTIC ROCK	00699577 / $15.95	
VOL. 20 – ROCKABILLY	00699580 / $17.99	
VOL. 21 – SANTANA	00174525 / $17.99	
VOL. 22 – CHRISTMAS	00699600 / $15.99	
VOL. 23 – SURF	00699635 / $17.99	
VOL. 24 – ERIC CLAPTON	00699649 / $19.99	
VOL. 25 – THE BEATLES	00198265 / $19.99	
VOL. 26 – ELVIS PRESLEY	00699643 / $16.99	
VOL. 27 – DAVID LEE ROTH	00699645 / $16.95	
VOL. 28 – GREG KOCH	00699646 / $19.99	
VOL. 29 – BOB SEGER	00699647 / $16.99	
VOL. 30 – KISS	00699644 / $17.99	
VOL. 32 – THE OFFSPRING	00699653 / $14.95	
VOL. 33 – ACOUSTIC CLASSICS	00699656 / $19.99	
VOL. 35 – HAIR METAL	00699660 / $17.99	
VOL. 36 – SOUTHERN ROCK	00699661 / $19.99	
VOL. 37 – ACOUSTIC UNPLUGGED	00699662 / $22.99	
VOL. 38 – BLUES	00699663 / $17.99	
VOL. 39 – '80s METAL	00699664 / $17.99	
VOL. 40 – INCUBUS	00699668 / $17.95	
VOL. 41 – ERIC CLAPTON	00699669 / $17.99	
VOL. 42 – COVER BAND HITS	00211597 / $16.99	
VOL. 43 – LYNYRD SKYNYRD	00699681 / $22.99	
VOL. 44 – JAZZ GREATS	00699689 / $19.99	
VOL. 45 – TV THEMES	00699718 / $14.95	
VOL. 46 – MAINSTREAM ROCK	00699722 / $16.95	
VOL. 47 – JIMI HENDRIX SMASH HITS	00699723 / $22.99	
VOL. 48 – AEROSMITH CLASSICS	00699724 / $19.99	
VOL. 49 – STEVIE RAY VAUGHAN	00699725 / $17.99	
VOL. 50 – VAN HALEN: 1978-1984	00110269 / $19.99	
VOL. 51 – ALTERNATIVE '90s	00699727 / $14.99	
VOL. 52 – FUNK	00699728 / $15.99	
VOL. 53 – DISCO	00699729 / $14.99	
VOL. 54 – HEAVY METAL	00699730 / $17.99	
VOL. 55 – POP METAL	00699731 / $14.95	
VOL. 57 – GUNS 'N' ROSES	00159922 / $19.99	
VOL. 58 – BLINK 182	00699772 / $17.99	
VOL. 59 – CHET ATKINS	00702347 / $17.99	
VOL. 60 – 3 DOORS DOWN	00699774 / $14.95	
VOL. 62 – CHRISTMAS CAROLS	00699798 / $12.95	
VOL. 63 – CREEDENCE CLEARWATER REVIVAL	00699802 / $17.99	
VOL. 64 – ULTIMATE OZZY OSBOURNE	00699803 / $19.99	
VOL. 66 – THE ROLLING STONES	00699807 / $19.99	
VOL. 67 – BLACK SABBATH	00699808 / $17.99	
VOL. 68 – PINK FLOYD – DARK SIDE OF THE MOON	00699809 / $17.99	
VOL. 71 – CHRISTIAN ROCK	00699824 / $14.95	
VOL. 74 – SIMPLE STRUMMING SONGS	00151706 / $19.99	
VOL. 75 – TOM PETTY	00699882 / $19.99	
VOL. 76 – COUNTRY HITS	00699884 / $16.99	
VOL. 77 – BLUEGRASS	00699910 / $17.99	
VOL. 78 – NIRVANA	00700132 / $17.99	
VOL. 79 – NEIL YOUNG	00700133 / $24.99	
VOL. 81 – ROCK ANTHOLOGY	00700176 / $22.99	
VOL. 82 – EASY ROCK SONGS	00700177 / $17.99	
VOL. 83 – SUBLIME	00369114 / $17.99	
VOL. 84 – STEELY DAN	00700200 / $19.99	
VOL. 85 – THE POLICE	00700269 / $17.99	
VOL. 86 – BOSTON	00700465 / $19.99	
VOL. 87 – ACOUSTIC WOMEN	00700763 / $14.99	
VOL. 88 – GRUNGE	00700467 / $16.99	
VOL. 89 – REGGAE	00700468 / $15.99	
VOL. 90 – CLASSICAL POP	00700469 / $14.99	
VOL. 91 – BLUES INSTRUMENTALS	00700505 / $19.99	
VOL. 92 – EARLY ROCK INSTRUMENTALS	00700506 / $17.99	
VOL. 93 – ROCK INSTRUMENTALS	00700507 / $17.99	
VOL. 94 – SLOW BLUES	00700508 / $16.99	
VOL. 95 – BLUES CLASSICS	00700509 / $15.99	
VOL. 96 – BEST COUNTRY HITS	00211615 / $16.99	
VOL. 97 – CHRISTMAS CLASSICS	00236542 / $14.99	
VOL. 99 – ZZ TOP	00700762 / $17.99	
VOL. 100 – B.B. KING	00700466 / $16.99	
VOL. 101 – SONGS FOR BEGINNERS	00701917 / $14.99	
VOL. 102 – CLASSIC PUNK	00700769 / $14.99	
VOL. 104 – DUANE ALLMAN	00700846 / $22.99	
VOL. 105 – LATIN	00700939 / $16.99	
VOL. 106 – WEEZER	00700958 / $17.99	
VOL. 107 – CREAM	00701069 / $17.99	
VOL. 108 – THE WHO	00701053 / $17.99	
VOL. 109 – STEVE MILLER	00701054 / $19.99	
VOL. 110 – SLIDE GUITAR HITS	00701055 / $17.99	
VOL. 111 – JOHN MELLENCAMP	00701056 / $14.99	
VOL. 112 – QUEEN	00701052 / $16.99	
VOL. 113 – JIM CROCE	00701058 / $19.99	
VOL. 114 – BON JOVI	00701060 / $17.99	
VOL. 115 – JOHNNY CASH	00701070 / $17.99	
VOL. 116 – THE VENTURES	00701124 / $17.99	
VOL. 117 – BRAD PAISLEY	00701224 / $16.99	
VOL. 118 – ERIC JOHNSON	00701353 / $19.99	
VOL. 119 – AC/DC CLASSICS	00701356 / $19.99	
VOL. 120 – PROGRESSIVE ROCK	00701457 / $14.99	
VOL. 121 – U2	00701508 / $17.99	
VOL. 122 – CROSBY, STILLS & NASH	00701610 / $16.99	
VOL. 123 – LENNON & McCARTNEY ACOUSTIC	00701614 / $16.99	
VOL. 124 – SMOOTH JAZZ	00200664 / $17.99	
VOL. 125 – JEFF BECK	00701687 / $19.99	
VOL. 126 – BOB MARLEY	00701701 / $17.99	
VOL. 127 – 1970s ROCK	00701739 / $17.99	
VOL. 129 – MEGADETH	00701741 / $17.99	
VOL. 130 – IRON MAIDEN	00701742 / $17.99	
VOL. 131 – 1990s ROCK	00701743 / $14.99	
VOL. 132 – COUNTRY ROCK	00701757 / $15.99	
VOL. 133 – TAYLOR SWIFT	00701894 / $16.99	
VOL. 135 – MINOR BLUES	00151350 / $17.99	
VOL. 136 – GUITAR THEMES	00701922 / $14.99	
VOL. 137 – IRISH TUNES	00701966 / $17.99	
VOL. 138 – BLUEGRASS CLASSICS	00701967 / $17.99	
VOL. 139 – GARY MOORE	00702370 / $17.99	
VOL. 140 – MORE STEVIE RAY VAUGHAN	00702396 / $24.99	
VOL. 141 – ACOUSTIC HITS	00702401 / $16.99	
VOL. 142 – GEORGE HARRISON	00237697 / $17.99	
VOL. 143 – SLASH	00702425 / $19.99	
VOL. 144 – DJANGO REINHARDT	00702531 / $17.99	
VOL. 145 – DEF LEPPARD	00702532 / $19.99	
VOL. 146 – ROBERT JOHNSON	00702533 / $16.99	
VOL. 147 – SIMON & GARFUNKEL	14041591 / $19.99	
VOL. 148 – BOB DYLAN	14041592 / $17.99	
VOL. 149 – AC/DC HITS	14041593 / $19.99	
VOL. 150 – ZAKK WYLDE	02501717 / $19.99	
VOL. 151 – J.S. BACH	02501730 / $16.99	
VOL. 152 – JOE BONAMASSA	02501751 / $24.99	
VOL. 153 – RED HOT CHILI PEPPERS	00702990 / $22.99	
VOL. 155 – ERIC CLAPTON UNPLUGGED	00703085 / $17.99	
VOL. 156 – SLAYER	00703770 / $19.99	
VOL. 157 – FLEETWOOD MAC	00101382 / $19.99	
VOL. 159 – WES MONTGOMERY	00102593 / $22.99	
VOL. 160 – T-BONE WALKER	00102641 / $17.99	
VOL. 161 – THE EAGLES ACOUSTIC	00102659 / $19.99	
VOL. 162 – THE EAGLES HITS	00102667 / $19.99	
VOL. 163 – PANTERA	00103036 / $19.99	
VOL. 164 – VAN HALEN: 1986-1995	00110270 / $19.99	
VOL. 165 – GREEN DAY	00210343 / $17.99	
VOL. 166 – MODERN BLUES	00700764 / $16.99	
VOL. 167 – DREAM THEATER	00111938 / $24.99	
VOL. 168 – KISS	00113421 / $17.99	
VOL. 169 – TAYLOR SWIFT	00115982 / $16.99	
VOL. 170 – THREE DAYS GRACE	00117337 / $16.99	
VOL. 171 – JAMES BROWN	00117420 / $16.99	
VOL. 172 – THE DOOBIE BROTHERS	00119670 / $17.99	
VOL. 173 – TRANS-SIBERIAN ORCHESTRA	00119907 / $19.99	
VOL. 174 – SCORPIONS	00122119 / $19.99	
VOL. 175 – MICHAEL SCHENKER	00122127 / $19.99	
VOL. 176 – BLUES BREAKERS WITH JOHN MAYALL & ERIC CLAPTON	00122132 / $19.99	
VOL. 177 – ALBERT KING	00123271 / $17.99	
VOL. 178 – JASON MRAZ	00124165 / $17.99	
VOL. 179 – RAMONES	00127073 / $17.99	
VOL. 180 – BRUNO MARS	00129706 / $16.99	
VOL. 181 – JACK JOHNSON	00129854 / $16.99	
VOL. 182 – SOUNDGARDEN	00138161 / $17.99	
VOL. 183 – BUDDY GUY	00138240 / $17.99	
VOL. 184 – KENNY WAYNE SHEPHERD	00138258 / $17.99	
VOL. 185 – JOE SATRIANI	00139457 / $19.99	
VOL. 186 – GRATEFUL DEAD	00139459 / $17.99	
VOL. 187 – JOHN DENVER	00140839 / $19.99	
VOL. 188 – MÖTLEY CRÜE	00141145 / $19.99	
VOL. 189 – JOHN MAYER	00144350 / $19.99	
VOL. 190 – DEEP PURPLE	00146152 / $19.99	
VOL. 191 – PINK FLOYD CLASSICS	00146164 / $17.99	
VOL. 192 – JUDAS PRIEST	00151352 / $19.99	
VOL. 193 – STEVE VAI	00156028 / $19.99	
VOL. 194 – PEARL JAM	00157925 / $17.99	
VOL. 195 – METALLICA: 1983-1988	00234291 / $22.99	
VOL. 196 – METALLICA: 1991-2016	00234292 / $19.99	

Prices, contents, and availability subject to change without notice.

HAL•LEONARD®
www.halleonard.com

0822
173

ESSENTIAL ELEMENTS FOR GUITAR

Essential Elements Comprehensive Guitar Method

Take your guitar teaching to a new level! With popular songs in a variety of styles, and quality demonstration and backing tracks on the accompanying online audio, *Essential Elements for Guitar* is a staple of guitar teachers' instruction – and helps beginning guitar students off to a great start. This method was designed to meet the National Standards for Music Education, with features such as cross-curricular activities, quizzes, multicultural songs, basic improvisation and more.

BOOK 1
by Will Schmid and Bob Morris

Concepts covered in Book 1 include: getting started; basic music theory; guitar chords; notes on each string; music history; ensemble playing; performance spotlights; and much more! Songs include: Dust in the Wind • Eleanor Rigby • Every Breath You Take • Hey Jude • Hound Dog • Let It Be • Ode to Joy • Rock Around the Clock • Stand by Me • • Sweet Home Chicago • This Land Is Your Land • You Really Got Me • more!

| 00862639 | Book/Online Audio | $19.99 |
| 00001173 | Book Only | $14.99 |

BOOK 2
by Bob Morris

Concepts taught in Book 2 include: playing melodically in positions up the neck; movable chord shapes up the neck; scales and extended chords in different keys; fingerpicking and pick style; improvisation in positions up the neck; and more! Songs include: Auld Lang Syne • Crazy Train • Folsom Prison Blues • La Bamba • Landslide • Nutcracker Suite • Sweet Home Alabama • Your Song • and more.

| 00865010 | Book/Online Audio | $22.99 |
| 00120873 | Book Only | $14.99 |

Essential Elements Guitar Ensembles

The songs in the Essential Elements Guitar Ensemble series are playable by three or more guitars. Each arrangement features the melody, a harmony part, and bass line in standard notation along with chord symbols. For groups with more than three or four guitars, the parts can be doubled. This series is perfect for classroom guitar ensembles or other group guitar settings.

Mid-Beginner Level
EASY POP SONGS
00865011/$10.99

CHRISTMAS CLASSICS
00865015/$9.99

CHRISTMAS SONGS
00001136/$10.99

Late Beginner Level
CLASSICAL THEMES
00865005/$10.99

POP HITS
00001128/$12.99

ROCK CLASSICS
00865001/$10.99

Early Intermediate Level
J.S. BACH
00123103/$9.99

THE BEATLES
00172237/$12.99

CHRISTMAS FAVORITES
00128600/$12.99

DISNEY SONGS
00865014/$14.99

IRISH JIGS & REELS
00131525/$9.99

JAZZ BALLADS
00865002/$14.99

MULTICULTURAL SONGS
00160142/$9.99

POPULAR SONGS
00241053/$12.99

TOP SONGS 2010-2019
00295218/$9.99

Mid-Intermediate Level
THE BEATLES
00865008/$14.99

BOSSA NOVA
00865006/$12.99

CHRISTMAS CLASSICS
00865015/$9.99

DUKE ELLINGTON
00865009/$9.99

GREAT THEMES
00865012/$10.99

JIMI HENDRIX
00865013/$9.99

JAZZ STANDARDS
00865007/$14.99

ROCK HITS
00865017/$12.99

ROCK INSTRUMENTALS
00123102/$9.99

TOP HITS
00130606/$9.99

Late Intermediate to Advanced Level
JAZZ CLASSICS
00865016/$9.99

Essential Elements Guitar Songs

The books in the Essential Elements Guitar Songs series feature popular songs selected for the practice of specific guitar chord types. Each book includes eight songs and a CD with fantastic sounding play-along tracks. Practice at any tempo with the included Amazing Slow Downer software!

BARRE CHORD ROCK
00001137   Late-Beginner Level $12.99

POWER CHORD ROCK
00001139   Mid-Beginner Level $16.99

More Resources

DAILY GUITAR WARM-UPS
by Tom Kolb
Mid-Beginner to Late Intermediate
00865004 Book/Online Audio $14.99

GUITAR FLASH CARDS
96 Cards for Beginning Guitar
00865000..$12.99

HAL•LEONARD®
www.halleonard.com